D0711444

FUNTASTICS

FUN AND GAMES
PEOPLE PLAY

by Louis O. Inks

G/L
REGAL
BOOKS
™

A Division of G/L Publications
Glendale, California, U.S.A.

Published by
Regal Books Division, G/L Publications
Glendale, California 91209, U.S.A.

Library of Congress Catalog Card No. (applied for)
ISBN 0-8307-0144-3

Contents

Unless otherwise designated, games are suitable
for both junior and high school youth
groups. A few games are suggested for just one
age group and are designated in the book as
JH (junior high) and HS (high school).

Foreword

After twelve years of youth work and research of over one hundred game books and assorted sources, I have come with pen in hand!

Why a new game book? Most books contain only a few games that will appeal to youth. The average person does not have the time to read or the money to buy all these books, only to find a "few" usable games in each.

Perhaps you have discovered that just any old game will not do when it comes to teens. Also, you have probably run the old favorites into the ground.

FUNTASTICS is a collection of fun ideas that have been tested and found successful with teens. There are enough games in this book to keep your teens in fun for a year.

Is FUN a waste of time?

Not if you want to win youth!

The first step toward conducting successful socials is to realize the importance of having them.

Teens will seek to satisfy their God-implanted social instinct. They are caught up in a social vortex and the church should take advantage of this characteristic.

Before we can win—build—and send youth, we need to attract them! The fun times can be a beginning in this direction. The world of youth tends to look down on the church as "dullsville." The church begins to lose her grip on them when she fails to appeal to the well-rounded life—physical, social and spiritual. "Spin the bottle" will not do. The world offers class . . . what do YOU offer? That is . . . IF you have their attention!

The vital church ministers to every aspect of the teen-ager's life . . . spiritual, social, emotional and physical. The latter three can be met to a degree through a well-planned social-recreational program. A well-planned social activity paves the way to making the teen a better listener when it is time for a spiritual impact. This does not mean that the spiritual and the social can be separated. Christ should be, and indeed must be, a part of all that we do.

How to Succeed

HOW TO DO IT TIPS FOR THE LEADER

HOW TO SUCCEED

Planning and producing a teen social calls for good judgment, cold realism and a few keen psychological insights. If you urge a group of one hundred to turn out en masse for a function which is really interesting to only twenty teens, the eighty who stayed away will feel guilty and negative about the activity that they are deliberately skipping. The interested twenty who attended will look at the empty seats and puny crowd and call the activity a flop. Let me clarify at this point that numbers do not determine success or failure. Certain activities attended by a handful of four or five can be a smashing success. Other activities which are overpublicized, poorly programmed, and heavily attended can realistically be called flops.

Do not attempt to make every function the biggest or the most exciting. Social activities can be divided into three classes:

The Type "C" social is a tiny get-together, often thrown together on the spur of the moment.

It is spontaneous and inexpensive. It is a simple and natural experience of Christian fellowship.

The Type **"B"** social is bigger. It involves a large number of teens. It is an attempt to attract a moderate percentage of the total group. "B" functions call for the three "P's—planning, publicity and program. This type of activity is held about twice every three months.

The Type **"A"** social function pulls out all stops. It is a special activity planned to attract and delight the entire group plus a large number of outsiders. It occurs only two or three times a year.

PARTY PREPARATION

In organizing a party it is important to involve as many persons as possible in carefully chosen, functioning committees. You will find this the most important factor in making a type "A" or "B" function succeed. Ask many individuals to take on specific responsibilities, but do not manufacture "busy work." (You will find that it causes many frustrations rather than satisfactions.) To insure the greatest success, plan with your teens and not for them.

Most parties will need committees to perform five basic functions: publicity, decorations, program, refreshments and cleanup. Your motto should be: Proper prior planning prevents pitifully poor performance.

Publicity

The purpose of publicity is to whet the appetite and to create interest in the coming social event. You will discover that a personal invitation designed for a definite commitment usually produces the best results. However, printed invitations, posters, verbal announcements and skits may be used very effectively.

It is important to begin publicizing far enough in advance for all those concerned to keep the date clear on their calendars. Three or more weeks are needed to do an adequate job of publicizing.

The publicity should include the following information: (1) the kind of social (e.g., swimming, ski retreat, formal banquet), (2) the date, (3) time, (4) place, (5) cost, (6) proper dress for the occasion and (7) the deadline for signing up.

When you plan refreshments and other supplies it is always helpful to know how many teens are going to attend. This is accomplished by "jacking" the price of the party up $1 and setting a sign-up deadline. All those who sign up and pay before the deadline (usually one week in advance), get a bargain price—$1 off. Those who sign up after the deadline have to pay the inflated price.

Decorations

Decorations help you to create a party atmosphere that promises a new and stimulating experience. That first impression a teen receives upon arrival is most important! The atmosphere of an inviting room seems to say "Hi! It's great to have you here! This is going to be FANTASTIC!" From that moment on, your teen will feel welcome and will anticipate the good time you have in store for him.

Here are some helpful ideas for you as you begin your task of decorating:

The most obvious way to begin would be to build your decorations around a season or holiday (such as Lincoln's Birthday, Valentine's Day, Christmas or fall).

Full-length wall murals encourage party-goers to respond to the kind of party you have planned (outdoor scenery, football player, hearts and flowers or other appropriate themes).

A rotating color wheel focused on your wall mural will bring "Ooooooos" and "Ahhhhhhhs." The use of black lighting and fluorescent paints can highlight those areas to which you want to draw attention.

Use artificial lighting by hanging small Christmas tree lights from the ceiling to simulate twinkling stars.

A simple indoor waterfall can be created by placing a ladder at a forty-five degree angle with one side resting in a large tub. Cover the ladder and "works" with heavy plastic, punching in the plastic between the rungs so the water will "ripple" as it descends. A circulating pump with two lengths of garden hose will keep your water going down, around and up to the top again all evening.

Felt tip pens (washable ink) can be used to decorate feet at a shoeless party!

Old newspapers can be used to make hats, and will add to the decorations you have already prepared.

Department stores, grocery stores and other places of business which regularly set up advertising displays, often throw away materials which are ideal for decorating. Make friends with the managers and let them know what kind of decorations you can use throughout the year.

Program

A suggested outline:
1. Preparty activity
2. Icebreaker
3. Musical mixer game
4. Relay
5. Stunt
6. Active game
7. Quiet game
8. Refreshments
9. Group singing
10. Serious closing

A good party is one in which the program is developed to meet the needs and the tastes of those who will attend. Consider the possibility that some teens will arrive early and be prepared to have them help you with the last minute arrangements. The party should begin the moment the first teen walks through the door.

At a small party personal introductions are made. At a large party name tags and mixer games help teens to become acquainted. Name tags not only help them to remember the names of new acquaintances but eliminate those uncomfortable moments when an individual forgets the name of a good friend.

A preparty game should create instant fun. In choosing an activity that will serve as a preparty game, use one that gets them into the fun in a hurry. It should be a game that a few can begin and that others may easily join as they arrive.

After the preparty activities and a game or two for getting acquainted, select a number of both active and quiet games. Organize them with a proper balance so that an energetic group will have plenty of activity with an occasional quiet game. The quiet game is to allow them to catch their breath. For variety mix in a stunt, trick or mind teaser. Always be prepared with more games than you will have time to use.

Timing is the key to the execution of a successful party. Remember that one or two of your games may not click. The moment you realize that you have a loser, change quickly. Keep in mind that some games will not take as long to play as you estimated. The speed of individual games should keep things rolling along so that there are no awkward pauses. Never let a particular game become routine. A game, as well as a party, should always end when everyone is at the peak of excitement. Ending in such a positive way will cause teens to clamor for the next activity and will never leave you with a flop on your hands. This sensitivity to timing is a "sixth sense" that you can develop with time and experience.

Games should be foolproof. They should carry themselves along with their own fun without depending too much on individual talent or wit. Few persons are innately clever enough to make up a funny play or speech on the spur of the moment. Any way you look at it, if you want to be successful, spell it "work." No easiest way method succeeds. You must always keep them guessing as to what is coming. If you do this, you are bound to plan, plan, plan and work, work, work!

Your leadership determines the quality of your social. To be an effective leader you will find these general principles helpful:

1. Approach the task prayerfully.

2. Plan ahead! Weeks in advance of your social you should be gathering materials, practicing the skits with the teens who will be involved, lining up your games, ordering refreshments and securing a room. The social will be a greater success if you can enter the party knowing that all these things are taken care of!

3. Learn to delegate responsibility. One of the fastest ways to multiply yourself is to take several teens into your confidence and have them execute the party with you, directing them in ways of leadership.

4. Learn and practice the principles of group dynamics. Place yourself in a position where you can be heard and seen by everyone. Use a voice that can be heard by all and of such a quality to command attention. If your voice is weak, then a megaphone or some type of P.A. system should be used.

Always make sure everyone understands what is happening and that there are no questions. On difficult games where you are divided into large groups, written instructions should be handed to the leaders of the teams or in some cases to everyone.

During the game, maintain total control by placing yourself where all can continue to hear and see you. A megaphone or P.A. system at this point will help you to maintain control of a large group. Have the backs of your teens turned to any who might come in late, thereby eliminating chance of distraction.

Have your props close at hand and in order; this eliminates awkward pauses. Some kind of box with manila folders for filing will help you to move more quickly through your activity.

Don't allow your game to lose momentum, but stop at the peak of excitement. Since timing is important and you're not able to foresee all that will happen, it is important that you be prepared for an emergency in your schedule or in the actual transaction of an activity. This book should be read carefully and several games tucked away in your memory which you could pull out and use at a moment's notice. Always prepare a few games appropriate for a different location or time of day in case the weather forces a schedule change.

A game resource box with balloons, string, scissors, tape, paper, pencils and props needed for your emergency games will come in handy.

The use of prizes or awards during the party can easily be given either to individuals or a team.

This can best be done by giving points for each game. It is better group dynamics to give 1,000 points rather than 100 points for a given game, and to have 75,000 points amassed at the end of the evening rather than 750 points. The awards can be in the form of a booby prize for the loser, like some idiotic thing to allow laughter for the winning team. The losers can be made to crank the handles of the ice cream makers or to clean up afterwards. They can also be made to "run the gamut." (The winning team has rolled-up newspapers in their hands while standing in a double line. The losers run through the two lines as the newspapers are swung at them, dodging either way without touching those with the newspapers.)

If you add enthusiasm to work on the part of those in charge, you'll have a sure formula for party success anywhere, any time, under any condition. Fun is an attitude rather than an activity. Ooooooze enthusiasm . . . it's catchy!

Crowd Warmers

CROWD WARMERS

The object of Crowd Warmers is to help individuals get acquainted and help them have an exciting time. These games should be scheduled early in the program.

Getting acquainted or better acquainted is an important factor of all games and play, but there are some games that help accomplish this more quickly than others. When there is the least doubt about the people knowing each other's names, it is important to provide some system of name cards or tags.

BINGO MIXER

Each player is given a card showing a diagram of squares. The number of squares on each card corresponds to the number of persons present. The diagram consists of the required number of squares in horizontal rows. The player then gets the autographs of all the others, one autograph in each square. When all autographs have been obtained, the leader calls names at random from slips drawn from a bowl or a hat. As each name is called the players check it off on their cards and the first one to check all the names in any horizontal row is the winner.

AMNESIA (famous characters)

Prepare beforehand slips on which are written the names of famous people, both present-day and historical. As each guest enters pin a slip on his back without letting him know what it says. The guests observe each other's slips and then converse with one another as though they were talking with the person named on the slip. As this goes on each tries to guess who he is supposed to be. The remarks should not be so leading as to give away the identity too soon. Much interesting and amusing conversation will ensue. (HS)

STRING-MANIA

This is a puzzle teaser and is good for an ice-breaker. Cut two thirty-six-inch pieces of string and tie one end to the right wrist and the other to the left. Repeat the process on your partner, but before tying it cross the strings. The object is to untangle the strings without breaking them. It can be done!

Solution: Make a loop in your string and slide it under the string tied around your partner's wrist and over his hand and presto, you're free. People will do everything but stand on their heads before finding the simple answer.

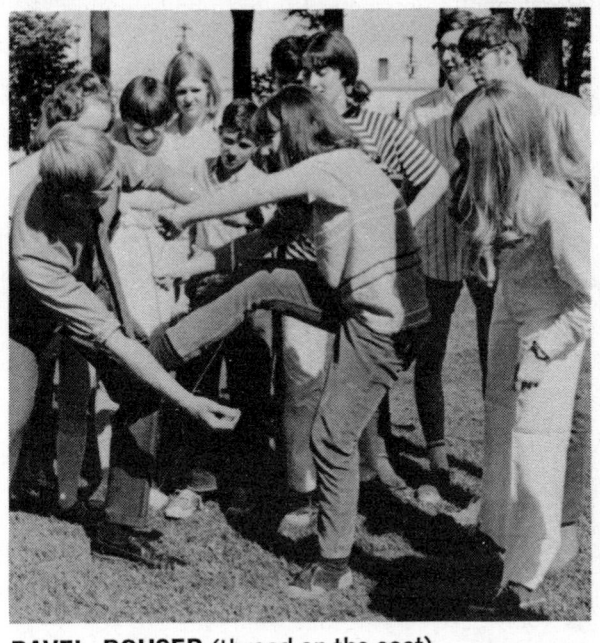

RAVEL ROUSER (thread on the coat)

The center of attraction in this stunt is the host. Each guest coming in, especially the ladies, will notice that the host has a white thread protruding through a seam on the back or shoulder of his dark suit. Someone will instinctively try to remove the thread, but the thread cannot be picked off or even snapped off. As the hapless guest pulls, the thread grows longer and longer, as if the whole suit were ravelling internally.

The host, of course, has a spool of thread in his inside pocket. He had previously threaded the end through a seam in his coat, removed the needle and left an inch or so of thread hanging.

Before new guests arrive, he cuts the dangling thread back so that only a short, inviting strand remains. The earlier guests watch with amusement as each newcomer yields to temptation and tries to remove the thread—and your party starts off on a humorous, ready-for-fun note.   (HS)

STOCKING-HEAD FREAKS

Even funnier looking than the faces you see in the amusement park's distorted mirrors are the faces you can produce with the aid of a stocking. Pull the top of an old nylon stocking down over your head and face. Pull it taut with one hand below your chin and the other hand stretching the stocking up over your face. The stretch of the stocking causes your features to stretch and flatten out with each pull. Before you play this game at your party try it out yourself. (If you wear glasses, remove them.)

Then, when game time arrives, stretch a sheet across a doorway at a height just a little above average chin level and hand each of your female guests a stocking. The boys stay on the other side of the sheet and do not see the girls until they put their heads over the top of the sheet. Then the boys try to guess their identities.

This will be surprisingly difficult, no matter how well they may know each other. The amount of distortion the stocking makes is almost unbelievable. In fact, by twisting and turning their stockings, grimacing and grinning, mugging and talking, the girls will make themselves so grotesque that no boy will want to admit acquaintance.

When the girls have finished their performance, the boys can try the same act. They will look just as freakish, if not more so.

CIRCLE COMBINES

Guests wander about the room as they choose. There is a loud call: "Make circles of . . . three and kneel."

Guests who are not part of a circle of three within one second are not penalized. To be left out seems penalty enough. The leader allows a few seconds for sociability within the circles, then calls, "Break up!" Each guest is on his own again until the next call, "Make circles of . . . five!" Or four, or six, or nine or any number. To bring the game to a climax, guests are asked to form circles of eleven for the last round. They never make it.

It is hard to understand why such simple action should create the laughter and determined competition it invariably does. Neither looks nor social position count with players trying to make a prescribed circle in the allotted time. They are without respect of persons when inducting a needed player or forcing out an extra.

CHAIN INTRODUCTIONS

The players stand or sit in a circle with the leader standing in the center. The leader, addressing the group as a whole, says, "How do you do? My name is Alice Jones," (giving her real name, of course). A designated player then walks up to Alice from his place in the circle and says, "How do you do, Alice Jones? My name is Jim Barnes." This cumulative process is continued, each person naming all those who have already introduced themselves and adding his own name, until some player fails. The game is then begun again with a new starter. The type of name used may vary with the situation. Instead of introducing herself as Alice Jones, a player might simply say Alice.

Each player must pronounce his name in such a way that all can hear and understand it. A good leader will not permit mumbling and will see to it that names are understood even if he has to spell them. Obviously this mixer has no place in a gathering where all players know each other well. (HS)

DOLLAR IN THE CROWD

This is a good mixer which will get everyone shaking hands. The leader or the committee in charge donates a dollar to the cause. This is given to someone in the group. The others do not, of course, know who holds it. The leader announces that the one holding the dollar will give it to the tenth person who shakes hands with him. Everyone at once begins shaking hands. The one who holds the dollar puts it in his pocket, keeps an accurate count and gives it to the tenth person who shakes hands with him. (Any number may be announced.)

If the group is large, give several quarters to the person and have him give one to each seventh person who shakes his hand.

ICEBREAKERS

Each guest on arrival is given a sheet of paper on which is written something for him to do. In doing this he will have to circulate among all the guests and speak to all as they come in. This is a dandy icebreaker and conversation maker. Here is a list of instructions to be given to your guests.

1. Count the brown-eyed boys in the room.

2. List the names of people who have seen a zebra.

3. Try to find out who knows what a flageolet is.

4. Try to find out who has made the longest trip and where to.

5. Find out who has the strangest hobby and what it is.

6. Ask every guest what was the most embarrassing situation he or she was ever in.

When the list is completed it is turned over to the hostess. When all the guests have arrived, the hostess reads the lists, much to the amusement of everyone.

SONG PARTNERS

Have the names of familiar songs written out in duplicate. Give one slip to each boy and one duplicate to each girl. At the signal from the leader all start singing or whistling their song. They try to find their partner who is whistling or singing the same song. This will create a lot of noise and fun. When the partners are found they cease singing.   (HS)

POSTCARD PUZZLES

Before the night of the party, cut several picture postcards into various shapes and put each piece in a separate envelope. Distribute the envelopes and give the group twenty minutes to sort themselves out according to picture and to put the puzzles together. Each postcard group is a natural team if you want to begin some relay games at this point.

ODD OR EVEN

Each person is given a dozen or so peanuts. The object is to get as many nuts from the others as possible. Bill goes up to Sue with a number of nuts concealed in his hand and says, "Odd or even?" Sue guesses, "Odd." Since there are seven peanuts in Bill's hand, she collects the seven nuts from him. If the guess had been wrong Sue would have had to turn seven peanuts over to Bill. A time limit is set and whoever has the most peanuts at the end wins a prize. When your peanuts are all gone, you're out!

PARTY WARM-UP

If you are having team competition, form teams by writing names of team members on individual slips of paper. Put the slips for each team in a different balloon and fill the balloons with helium. Let the balloons float to the ceiling, and when needed, turn the kids loose to get the balloons to find out which team they are on. (Balloons should be filled no more than an hour before party time or they will be on the floor instead of at the ceiling where they belong.)

THE CHIEF'S ORDERS

As the guests enter, give each girl an odd-numbered card and each fellow an even-numbered card. Each card reads: "The following are the Chief's orders, be sure to carry them out." Following are some suggested orders. Similar ones may be made up to suit the nature of the party and the interests of the group.   (HS)

1. You are the official introducer. Find number 2 and introduce him to number 12; number 4 and introduce him to number 10; number 6 to 8.

2. Same as the above with a boy introducing the girls.

3. Find number 16 and ask him to help you ask each boy who his favorite singer is. Later you will be asked to announce your results.

4. Find number 11 and ask her to help you ask each girl who her favorite singer is. Later you will be asked to announce your results.

5. Find number 14 and ask him to help you find out what each person's favorite T.V. program is. Later you will be asked to announce your results.

6. Find number 17 and together list the politics of everyone present.

7. Find number 12 and together ask each person what he or she considers the best song of the past year.

8. List all the blue-eyed girls.

9. List all the blue-eyed fellows.

10. List all the brown-eyed girls.

11. List all the brown-eyed fellows.

12. List all names that begin with "A."

MATCHING ADVERTISEMENTS

Cut advertisements from newspapers and magazines and cut each advertisement in half. As the guests enter give each one half of an advertisement. One half of each is given to a boy and the other half to a girl. Each guest finds the person who has the other half of his ad.

MATCHING WISDOM (old sayings)

Write old and well-known phrases on slips of paper and cut the slips in half. For example, take the phrase "strong as an ox." Cut it in two so that one slip reads "strong as an" and the other "ox."

Give the first part of it to a guy and the last part of it to a gal. They find the person who has the other half. (HS)

Strong as an ox	Still as a mouse
Poor as a church mouse	Fat as a pig
Mad as a wet hen	Black as coal
Plump as a partridge	Dry as a bone
Huge as an elephant	Fit as a fiddle
Funny as a monkey	Hard as a rock
Dead as a doornail	Swift as a hare
Flat as a pancake	White as snow
Clean as a whistle	Sweet as honey
Pretty as a picture	Tight as a drum
Quick as lightning	Sly as a fox
Slippery as an eel	Clear as crystal
Bright as the sun	Cold as ice
Tall as a giraffe	Thin as a rail
Light as a feather	Fair as a flower
Sharp as a razor	Ugly as sin
Crazy as a loon	Sour as a lemon
Red as a beet	Green as grass
Yellow as gold	Blind as a bat

SPLIT PROVERBS

Write out proverbs on slips of paper and cut each slip in half. There must be as many cut slips as there are guests expected. Give one half of a proverb to a guy and the other half to a gal. They locate partners by finding the person who has the other half of the proverb. For example, the boy's slip might read "is not gold" and the girl's "all that glitters." (HS)

25

A bad penny always comes back.

A barking dog never bites.

A bird in the hand is worth two in the bush.

A cloudy morning often changes to a fine day.

A friend in need is a friend indeed.

A fool and his money are soon parted.

A new broom sweeps clean.

A penny saved is a penny earned.

A person is known by the company he keeps.

A place for everything and everything in its place.

A rolling stone gathers no moss.

A stitch in time saves nine.

A watched pot never boils.

Absence makes the heart grow fonder.

All good things must come to an end.

All that glitters is not gold.

All's fair in love and war.

All's well that ends well.

An empty barrel makes the most noise.

Beggars should not be choosers.

Behind bad luck comes good luck.

Better late than never.

Birds of a feather flock together.

Contentment is better than riches.

Curiosity killed the cat.

Discretion is the better part of valor.

Early to bed and early to rise makes a man healthy, wealthy and wise.

Enough is as good as a feast.

Every cloud has a silver lining.

Everyone knows best where his shoe pinches him.

Everything comes to him who waits.

Evil to him who evil thinks.

Faint heart never won fair lady.

Forewarned is forearmed.

God helps those who help themselves.

Handsome is as handsome does.

He laughs best who laughs last.

Health is better than wealth.

Hitch your wagon to a star.

Honesty is the best policy.

Idleness is the mother of evil.

It never rains but it pours.

It takes a thief to catch a thief.

It takes two to make a quarrel.

It's a long lane that has no turning.

It's an ill wind that blows nobody good.

It's better to have loved and lost, than never to have loved at all.

It's the shovel that laughs at the poker.

Keep your eyes wide open before marriage, half shut afterwards.

Laugh and the whole world laughs with you; weep and you weep alone.

Lie down with the dogs, get up with the fleas.

Like father, like son.

Make hay while the sun shines.

Marry in haste, repent at leisure.

Necessity is the mother of invention.

Never look a gift horse in the mouth.

Never put off 'till tomorrow what can be done today.

No pay, no piper.

Nothing ventured, nothing gained.

Once does not make a habit.
One cannot please all the world and his wife.
One good turn deserves another.
Out of sight out of mind.
People in glass houses shouldn't throw stones.
Rome wasn't built in a day.
Silence gives consent.
Sorrow treads upon the heels of mirth.
Speech is silver, silence is golden.
Strike while the iron is hot.
Take care of the pennies, the dollars will take care of themselves.
The early bird catches the worm.
The pen is mightier than the sword.
The pot calls the kettle black.
The proof of the pudding is in the eating.
There are two sides to every question.
There's many a slip 'twixt the cup and the lip.
They can because they think they can.
To see an old friend is as agreeable as a good meal.
To the victor belong the spoils.
Too many cooks spoil the broth.
Two wrongs do not make a right.
Variety is the spice of life.
Wasteful waste makes woeful want.
Well done is better than well said.
Well done or not at all.
What's good for the goose is good for the gander.
When a man is wrapped up in himself, the package is small.
When in Rome, do as the Romans do.

Where there's a will there's a way.
Who counts without his host counts twice.
Who steals my purse steals trash.
You cannot have your cake and eat it too.
You may bring a horse to water, but you can't make him drink.

IDENTIFICATION OF PHOTOGRAPHS

Have each guest bring to the party a baby picture. These pictures are numbered and placed about the room or pinned to the curtains, etc. Each guest is given a slip of paper which is numbered with as many numbers as there are pictures. They guess the name and write it opposite the corresponding number. Give a prize to the one who has the largest number correct.   (JH)

SACK SHAKE

An ordinary paper sack is given to each guest on arrival. He must wear this sack on his right hand and shake hands with all the other guests while wearing it.

PROFILES

You will need one of your artists for this one. As each guest arrives he is taken into a room and asked to stand between a strong light and a smooth wall. Then the artist outlines his profile with a crayon, outlining only the head.

The artist is careful to write the name of each subject on the back of the drawings. When all guests have arrived the profiles are held up to see who can identify the most.

EYE SPY

In this mixer, everyone gets four pieces of paper and each is to list everyone in the room according to the color of his or her eyes. The first one to finish wins. (Each piece of paper is for an eye color: blue, green, brown, grey.)

SIT DOWN

Ask the entire audience to stand. Instruct them to sit down when the "if" characteristic applies to them and to remain seated. Encourage them to be as honest as possible. If you have trouble because most are not sitting down, then give some general characteristic, such as sit down if you are under fifteen (or over eighteen); sit down if you have white socks on; sit down if you are in love.

Sit down if:

You didn't use deodorant today.
You have worn the same socks for two days.
You sing in the shower.
Your bellybutton is an "outie."
You kiss with your eyes open.
You dated a loser this past weekend.
You are a boy and use hair spray.
You haven't taken a bath in a week.

You kiss sloppy.

You have a pimple on your nose.

You didn't use any mouthwash today.

You are a girl and haven't shaved your legs today.

You are a guy and did shave your legs today.

You still suck your thumb.

You wear "baby doll" pajamas.

Your nose is running and you don't have a handkerchief.

You are going steady but wish you weren't.

Your mother dresses you.

You have never been kissed.

You have ever "two-timed" your girlfriend or boyfriend.

LET'S GET ACQUAINTED

Print this form up and pass copies around to all your teens at the beginning of the party. Have them fill in other people's names in appropriate places.

1. Find someone who uses a tooth brightener. . . . .

2. Find someone who has three bathrooms in his house. . . . .

3. Find someone who has gotten more than two traffic tickets. . . . .

4. Find someone who has red hair. . . . .

5. Find someone who gets hollered at for spending too much time in the bathroom. . . . .

31

6. Find someone who has been inside the cockpit of an airplane. . . . .

7. Find someone who plays a guitar. . . . .
. . . .

8. Find someone who uses "Dippity-Do" hair goop. . . . .

9. Find someone who uses your brand of mouthwash. . . . .

10. Find someone who has used an outhouse. . . . .

11. Find a girl who is wearing false eyelashes. . . . .

12. Find a guy who has gone water skiing and got up the first time. . . . .

13. Find someone who is on a diet. . . . .

14. Find a girl who uses a Lady Remington shaver. . . . .

15. Find a guy who has a match with him. . . . .

16. Find someone who has his own private bath at home. . . . .

17. Find someone who didn't know your last name. . . . .

THE NOSE KNOWS

For this game you'll need paper and pencils for everyone and a dozen or so containers placed on a table with "smelly" things in them. Number each container and cover with some type of material (dark nylon stocking or cheesecloth) which hides the contents but allows the odor to come through. Tell teens to number their papers from

1-12 (or whatever number of containers you are using). Then let them smell contents of each container and write down what they think it is. Announce the winner later when you reveal the contents of the containers. Examples:

Ultra-Brite toothpaste
cigarette butts
pizza
fertilizer (animal)
mustard
Listerine mouthwash

tea
rotten eggs
vanilla extract
pair of dirty socks
different kinds of
    flowers or incense

CAN YOU FOLLOW INSTRUCTIONS?

Need pencils and printed copies of this sheet:

This is a timed test—you have five minutes only!

1. Read everything carefully before doing anything.

2. Put your name in the upper right-hand corner of this paper.

3. Circle the word NAME in sentence two.

4. Draw five small squares in the upper left-hand corner.

5. Put a circle around each square.

6. Put an "X" in each square.

7. Sign your name under the title of this paper.

8. After the title, write "YES, YES, YES."

9. Put an "X" in the lower left corner of this paper.

10. Put a circle completely around sentence and number seven.

11. Draw a triangle around the "X" you just put down.

12. On the back of this paper, multiply 703 x 66.

13. Draw a rectangle around the word "corner" in sentence four.

14. Loudly call out your first name when you get this far along.

15. If you think you have followed directions carefully to this point, call out, "I HAVE."

16. On the reverse side of this paper add 8,950 and 9,805.

17. Put a circle around your answer and put a square around the circle.

18. In your normal speaking voice, count from ten to one backwards.

19. Punch three small holes in the top of this paper with your pencil point.

20. If you are the first person to reach this point, loudly call out, "I AM THE FIRST PERSON TO REACH THIS POINT AND I AM THE LEADER IN THIS TEST!"

21. Underline all even numbers on the left side of this paper.

22. Put a square around each written-out number on this page.

23. Loudly call out, "I AM NEARLY FINISHED— I HAVE FOLLOWED INSTRUCTIONS."

24. Now that you have finished reading everything carefully, do only sentences one and two!

BALLOON BLAST

Have several hundred balloons on hand for this one. While half the crowd blows up the balloons the other half must keep them up in the air. The idea is to establish a world record for balloons being kept up in the air by a youth group. Any balloon that touches the floor has to be broken. If you give it a real big buildup, the kids will go for it! (JH)

A CAN STACK

A number of fellows from each team sees who can stack the highest stack of empty soup cans in a given amount of time.

Group Games

GROUP GAMES

Group games allow for total involvement either in physical activity or in laughing with the contestants. This assures everyone of a good time.

Important for Group Dynamics!

Place yourself in a position where you can be heard and seen by everyone.

Always make sure everyone understands what is happening and that there are no questions.

During the game maintain total control by placing yourself where all can continue to hear and see you.

Have the backs of the crowd to any who might arrive late, thereby limiting distraction.

Have your props close at hand and in order; this will eliminate awkward pauses.

Don't allow a game to lose momentum; stop at the peak of excitement.

LUCKY PENNY HUNT (a banquet stunt)

To liven things up during a banquet, have guests get out all the pennies they have with them and spread them on the table in front of them. Those who have fewer than five may buy five from the leader who has three or four saucers full of pennies on hand.

When all are ready to proceed, announce that certain pennies are lucky ones (six new pennies, a 1941, a 1901, a 1935, etc.) and entitle the holder to a prize.

BIRDIE ON THE PERCH

Have couples (at least 10) form two circles with boys on the outside and girls on the inside.

When the whistle blows, boys circle begins going clockwise and the girls counterclockwise. When the whistle blows again, the girls are to run to their partner (who crouches down with one knee on the ground) and jump up on his knee with her arms around his neck. The last couple to have the "birdie on the perch" is eliminated. The game continues until only one couple remains. (HS)

FURNITURE SMASH

Give each team an old piece of furniture, such as a chair, couch or piano that has been donated for this purpose, or was picked up at the Good Will. The idea is to see who can bust it up and pass the whole thing through a small hole that you cut out of a piece of plywood, or else put the entire smashed up item into a small cardboard box and close the lid.

BALLOON BURST

This is a hilarious affair. Give one guy a balloon and two feet of string. He inflates the balloon tightly and ties it to the left ankle of a girl. If possible, the balloons should be inflated beforehand and handed to the boys. The boy does not have a balloon. His responsibility is to protect his girl's balloon. Because of the tendency to seek an advantage by not inflating them completely, announce that all those balloons not fully inflated will be eliminated.

When the music starts all attempt to step on the balloons of others and at the same time defend their own. When a balloon is destroyed, the couple is eliminated. The couple remaining on the floor longest wins the prize.

BALLOON CONTEST

Each person receives an inflated balloon which he throws into the air, and tries to keep afloat as long as possible. While keeping his own balloon in the air he tries to beat other balloons to the floor. The object is to see whose balloon will stay in the air the longest.

This game may be played by individuals or competing couples. Couples receive only one balloon for the two of them.

GRABIT

Divide the group into two teams, one the de-stroyers and the other the defenders. A balloon is tossed up between them. The destroyers try to break the balloon by grabbing it, clapping their hands together on it or stepping on it, while the defenders attempt to protect it by batting it out of reach. Record the time required by the destroyers to break the balloon. When the balloon is broken, the defenders become the destroyers.

Give each team three turns at destroying the balloon. Add the times required by each team. The team with the smallest total time wins.

CROWS AND CRANES

Have two goal lines about 50 to 75 feet apart. Divide your contestants into equal teams, placing one team on each goal line. A leader stands near the center.

One team is called "Crows," and the other "Cranes." At a given signal from the leader both teams start marching toward each other. The leader will then cry "Cr-r-rows!" or he will cry "Cr-r-ranes!" Whichever team he calls must get back behind its goal without getting caught.

If he cries "Crows," then the cranes try to catch the crows. Everyone who is caught must go to the cranes' side. If he were to call "Cranes," then the crows would try to catch the cranes, with the same misfortune befalling those who were captured. To make the game more exciting the leader will occasionally give a false warning, using such words as "crackers," "crawfish," and the like. (JH)

KING OF THE CIRCLE

Mark off a big circle 10 feet in diameter or, if outside, dig a hole 2 feet deep and 10 feet in diameter and put about a dozen guys into it. At a given signal each tries to throw everybody else out while trying to stay in himself. The last guy to stay in the circle wins.

WATER BALLOON SHOT-PUT

A simple game to see who can put the "shot," a water balloon, the farthest. To give the game added incentive, the youth leader can stand at a place "just out of reach" of the shot-putters and they use him as a target.

AMERICAN EAGLE

This is one "ruff" game. Guys and gals play separately. All line up on a line except one who stands thirty feet or so away (in the middle of the field). When the whistle is blown, players start running toward the opposite side of the field, passing the guy in the middle. That guy tackles one (or more if he can), and has to hold him down and say "American Eagle" three times. The rest of the players now are on the other side of the field. Now they must run through the two or more guys to get back to the original side again. This keeps up until everybody has been tackled and is in the middle of the field. Give a prize to whoever lasts the longest.

A variation is to have the person in the middle pick up the runner he catches and hold him completely off the ground while shouting, "American Eagle, 1, 2, 3."

WILLIAM TELL

Construct two "candle hats" out of paper plates, ribbon and two short candles.

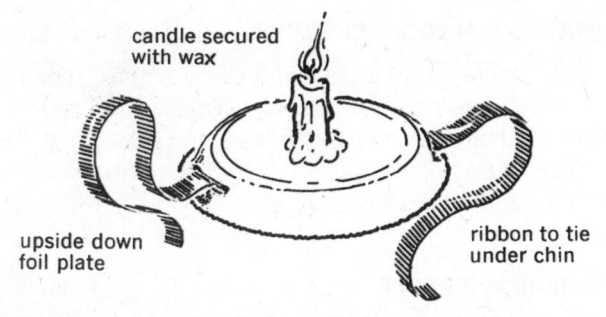

candle secured with wax

upside down foil plate

ribbon to tie under chin

Two guys get candles on their heads (they wear the above described candle hats) and they are given a squirt gun each. They get about 12 feet apart and have a duel to see who can squirt out the other guy's lighted candle first. The idea is to keep your candle lit and shoot the other guy's out.

A variation would be to use couples. Have two girls each get 10 or 15 feet away from their boyfriends and race to see who can put out their boyfriend's candle first. The guys just stand there and take a soaking.

WHEELBARROW EAT

Couples race "wheelbarrow" style. (Girls hold the guys' feet, guys walk on their hands.) They race to a goal but they must eat their way along the race course. (Place jelly beans, marshmallows or peanuts along the trail.)

STREETS AND ALLEYS

One person is IT and chases another person through a maze of people formed in this manner:

Everyone in the maze is facing in one direction with their hands joined, forming "alleys." When "streets" is called, all do a right face and grasp hands once more. The person who is IT tries to catch the runner and cannot cross the joined hands. When "alleys" is called, everyone in the maze assumes his original position.

CROSSWORD PEOPLE

Divide the group into teams of equal size. Prepare ahead of time sets of letters of the alphabet on large cards that each team member hangs around his neck. Each team should have identical sets of letters consisting of frequently used vowels and consonants, plus two or three rarely used letters such as Q, X or Z. At a signal each team tries to form a crossword puzzle, using as many of the team members as possible within given time limit.

Each team should have a captain who directs his team and keeps order. Award points for the team using the most of its members, the longest word or the most words. Another idea would be to assign a point value to each letter and add points up like you would if you were playing the game "Scrabble." (HS)

WATER BALLOON SHAVE

Three couples come up to the front of the room. The guys sit in chairs and hold a large water balloon on their heads. The girls cover the balloons with shaving cream and try to "shave" off all the shaving cream with a single-edged razor blade without breaking the balloon.

WINE MAKER

Get two washtubs and put grapes in each. Have two guys compete to see who can stomp the most juice out with their bare feet. Pour the juice into jars to measure the winner. Set a time limit and "threaten" to make the loser drink the other guy's juice. (Don't hold him to it, though . . .)

HUMAN TICKTACKTOE

Two equally divided teams are numbered off and face each other from left to right. A ticktacktoe diagram is drawn on the floor and numbers are called. When a number is called, that player from both teams runs to a square. The first one to a square keeps it. One team wins when it has a straight line of players to make a ticktacktoe. (HS)

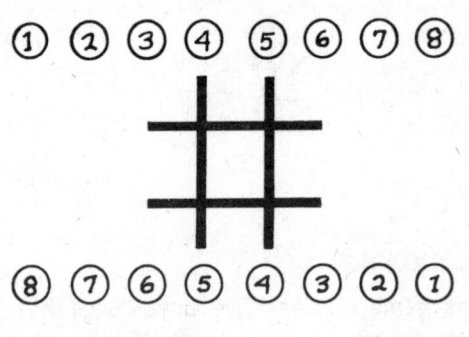

GIANT TWISTER

A "twister board" can be made by flattening out a large cardboard refrigerator box and painting it with circles of various colors. It is played like "Twister" of Milton and Bradley Toys. Everyone can play at the same time by placing several boxes together.

MASH THE HATS

Pick six boys to stand in a circle facing the back of the boy in front. Put a hat on all but one. When the leader yells "Go!" each boy takes the hat off the boy in front and puts it on his head repeating the process until the leader says "Stop!" The one without the hat is removed from the game as well as one of the hats to keep short one hat each time.

FOOT SIGNING

This game involves five boys. Each has three minutes to get as many signatures as possible on the bottom of one bare foot. Each girl may sign only four.   (HS)

BANANA SPLIT IN THE MOUTH

Have boys lie down on their backs while girls build a banana split in their wide-open mouths.

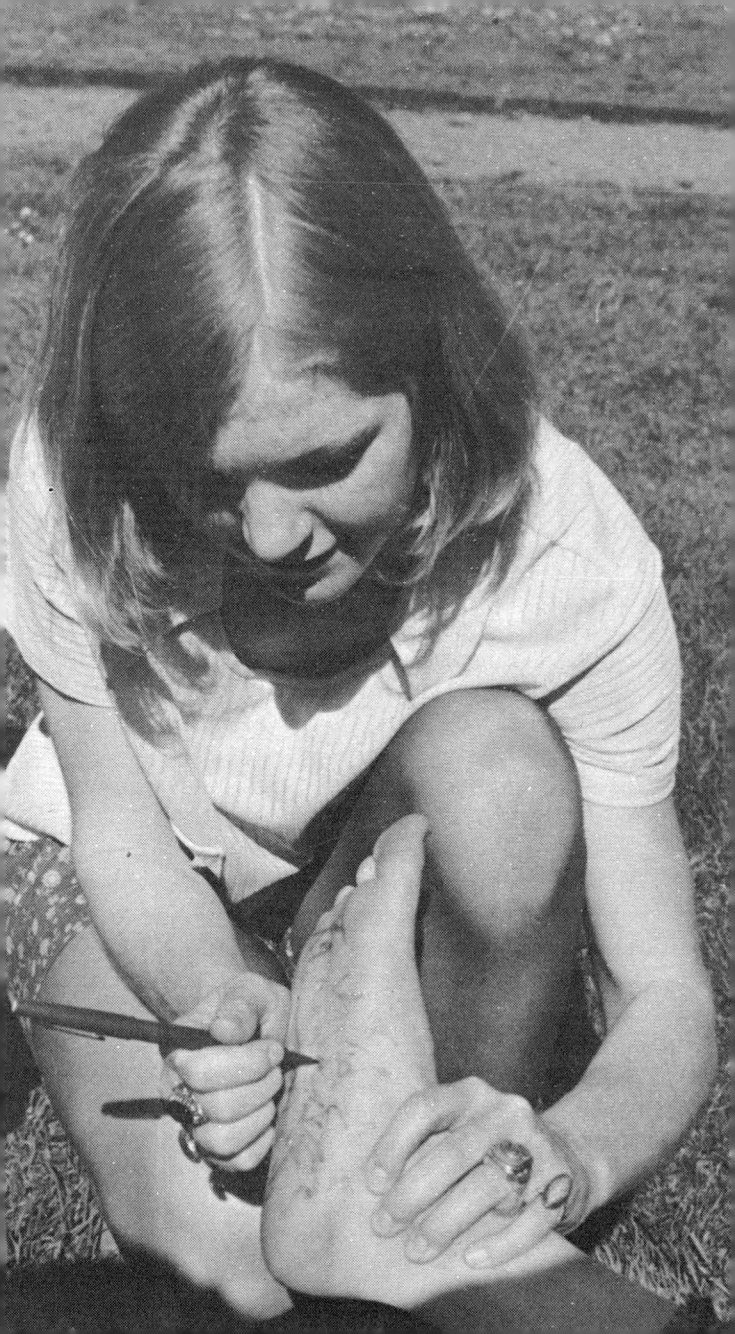

SCAVENGER HUNT

Make a list of items which the players may have in their possession (in pockets or purses) like combs, chewing gum, a sock with a hole in it, a certain color of lipstick and six blond hairs.

Divide the group into teams. Each team sends one of its members to the leader in the center of the room who whispers the name of an item into their ear. At the signal "Go!" they run back to their team and pantomime it until someone guesses and gives them the item which is immediately taken to the leader. The first one there with the item wins that round. Repeat the cycle.

RUSSIAN ROULETTE FOR CHICKEN HEARTS

Hard-boil four eggs and leave one raw (total of five eggs). Call up five boys. Each chooses the egg he wants broken on top of his head. One guy picks the raw egg and things get a little messy. For best results have five girls stand behind the guys and at a signal all five girls break the eggs simultaneously on each boy's head. (If you think this is too messy, poke a hole (small) in each end of the raw egg and blow the contents out. Fill the egg with water by drawing water into it like a straw. Cover each end where the holes are with a clear wax and you're in for a wet time!)

MARBLE FISH

Fill two pans full of crushed ice and have two guys try to fish out, with their bare toes, ten marbles placed on the bottom of the pan.

TIE-A-SHOE CONTEST

Three girls each tie a boy's shoe, using one hand and anything else (mouth, toe or heel).

OLIVE PACK

See who can get the most pitted olives in his mouth. Count them on their way IN. Make sure the guys don't swallow any.

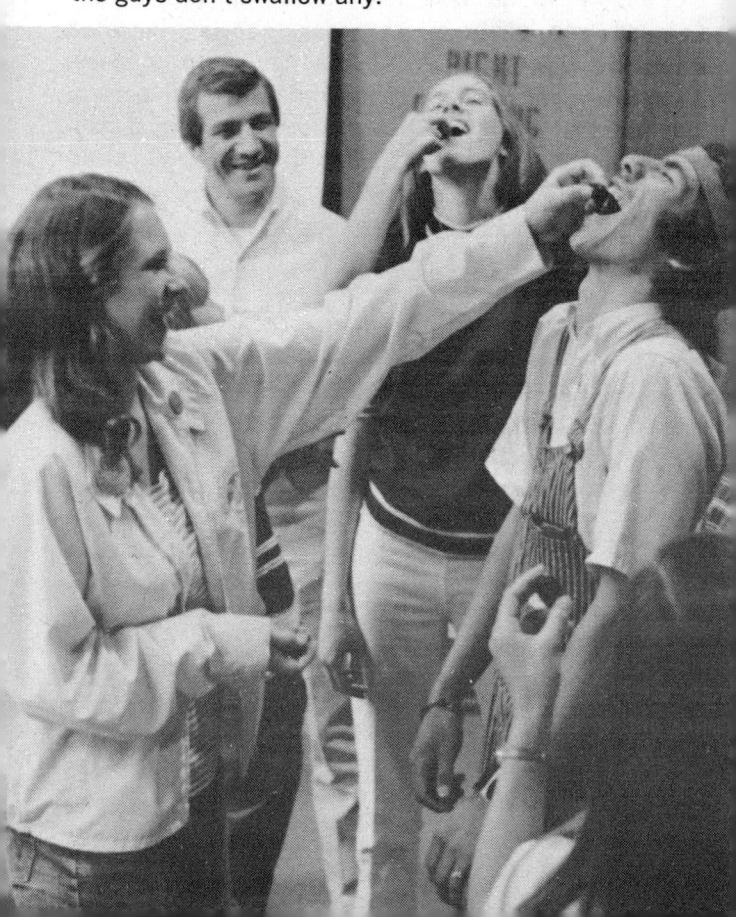

LAUGHING BALL

One player stands a short distance in front of the others who form a semicircle. The odd man has a rubber ball that he throws into the air and catches either as it descends or after one or more bounces from the floor. All the other players are required to laugh vigorously while the ball is out of the thrower's hands, but to be perfectly silent before he throws it and after he catches it. Anyone who laughs at the wrong time is eliminated and the process is repeated until only one remains. The game can easily be adapted to team scoring. A coin may be thrown instead of a ball, the laughing to cease when the coin lands head up on the floor.

MUMMY WRAP

This game or stunt is to have two teams or couples. Each team is handed a roll of toilet paper and a person from each team is selected to be the mummy. The team will take the paper and roll it around the mummy. The object is to wrap the mummy from his head to his feet without leaving any part of his body showing. The best-wrapped mummy wins. Hint: It is best to start with the feet and work up to the waist, then the head. Another way is to have a couple wrap themselves. They, too, should start by going around their feet and working up to the waist. They should cross or make an "X" over their shoulders making the wrap cover their heads next and work down to the

place where they left off around their waists. This is, of course, to leave their hands free until the last. After judging, "embalming" takes place by pouring water all over the guys wrapped in toilet paper.

WORD HUNT

Give each player a sheet of newspaper. The leader calls out certain words. The first one to find the word in his newspaper gets 100 points. Game is finished after 10 words have been tossed out to the group. Person with the highest number of points wins.   (HS)

WET A WAY TO GO

Put a cola bottle on a boy's forehead with him in a prone position (on his back) and have a girl fill it with water squeezed from a sponge. An alternate way would be to blindfold the girl and let her pour a cup of water into the bottle. Any way you do it, some bodies are going to be mighty wet. "Wet" a way to go!

WHO'S THE WEAKER SEX

The enthusiasm to be generated is dependent upon the leader in the introduction of this test. Follow each step of the introduction and pause just a moment for reaction.

"This is a test to see who is the strongest—the gals or the guys!

"I have drawn a square on the floor which I want all the guys to get into.

"Now, all you gals have to do is to drag, pull, push—I don't care how. But each time you get a guy out of the square you prove your superioity."

Now stand back a moment and wait for the reaction. Then add, "Oh, one last rule. Guys, you cannot resist the gals. The only thing you can do is to hold on to one another for dear life." It is better if they sit on the floor rather than stand.

TEMPTATION

About ten minutes before refreshment time each guest is given a deflated sausage-shaped balloon with a string attached to it. A card bearing a number is tied to the loose end of the string. Each guest blows up his balloon and pins it to his shoulder.

The balloons are "worn" during two or three active games. A player who cannot resist the temptation to touch off a neighbor's balloon with a pin is required to give up his balloon to that neighbor, provided the neighbor can produce two witnesses who saw the balloon touched off.

Just before refreshments are served, open warfare is declared. The person who keeps his balloon intact the longest wins a special prize. Then the cards that were attached to the balloons are produced and their values announced. Certain cards call for a minor prize; other numbers indicate service in the kitchen.

THIS IS MY EAR

Have your guests stand in a circle, with the exception of IT who stands in the center. IT points to anyone in the circle and, for example, touches his ear. However, he does not say, "This is my ear," but says, for example, "This is my elbow." The one to whom he has pointed must then point to his elbow and say, "This is my ear," while IT counts to ten. If he fails to do so, he becomes IT. If he succeeds, IT must try another person.

MIDNIGHT TUG OF WAR

Give your overnight retreats an unforgettable touch by having a tug of war at midnight under a floodlight. Dig a large "slime pit" (create slime with mud) and outline the tug of war area with a lime line. To add the finishing touch have a fire hose on full force across the pit through which they must be pulled.

RHYTHM

After everyone is seated in a circle the players start to beat time. They get a rhythm by slapping their hands on their knees, then clapping their hands together and then slapping their knees again. They keep this up until, at the last beat, someone starts the game by calling out a word.

For instance, player "A" calls out the word "good." The group then goes through the rhythm of clapping their knees, hands and knees. Right after the last motion the player sitting next to "A" in the circle must call out a word beginning with the last letter of the previous word. In this case the player can call out "dog." Then the group goes through the three rhythm motions again. Then the next player may call out "gift." If he had called out "good," he would have one point against him because words cannot be repeated.

This can be done with names. The person who starts the game calls out his name and the name of another player. The one whose name is called then says his name and another, etc.

The rhythm must be kept up this way: Clap, clap, clap, word; clap, clap, clap, word, etc. The game goes very quickly because the rhythm is fast. Names of persons and places cannot be used unless you are using them as a specific category. After a player misses three times, he is out of the game. A player can miss by giving the name of a person or place or by not giving any word directly after the last beat of the rhythm. (HS)

CARPET SOCCER

Using the living room carpet as your playing field and a balloon as the soccer ball, you can stage a soccer game throbbing with excitement. Limit your teams to four or five on a side, letting the remainder of the guests serve as the cheering section. Arm each contestant with a fan. The ball is moved across the field in either direction with a fan. Its progress can be retarded by the opposing team only with the use of a fan.

If anyone touches the ball in any way, either with his person or with the fan, his team is penalized half way to the goal line. Each time one team is able to fan the ball across the opposing goal line, that team chalks up a point.

BALLOON CORNER GOAL

The game is played with two balloons preferably twelve inches in diameter, one red and one blue, which are struck with the open hand only.

Players are divided into two teams designated by colors worn on the arm which correspond to the balloon colors. The teams are assigned by rows across the room from side to side. The first two people on each side belong to the red team, the second to the blue, the third to the red. Continue until everyone is on a team. Four goals are formed by stretching a tape diagonally across each of the four corners of the room about five feet above the floor. The goals in the diagonally opposite corners have the same colors, two of red and two of blue. The game consists of hitting the balloon with the open hand so that it will float down behind the goal tape, the red balloon scoring when it enters the red goals and the blue balloon when it enters the blue goals. There are no goal guards as it is the object of all players in each team to get their balloon into the appropriate goal while keeping the opponents from scoring with their balloon.

The game starts when the leaders put the balloons in play by tossing them up in the center of the room. Each side immediately begins to play for them. It has been found that with two balloons and four goals it is not necessary to limit the players to any given area. This, however, may be done should play become rough.

A scorekeeper scores ten points for each team making a goal with its balloon. Leaders put balloons back in play immediately after each goal. The game continues without interruption.   (HS)

BALLOON VOLLEY BALL

Divide the group into two sides. Select eight or ten from each group. If the whole group is not too large, let them all play. Stretch a string across the room about six feet above the floor. If the ceiling is high, it is better to have the string even higher than that. Inflate a balloon to use for the volley ball. Each side tries to keep the balloon from touching the floor on their side. If it touches the floor on their side the other side scores ten points. One hundred points make a game.

Another way to play this is to forbid the use of hands, allowing players to strike the ball only with their heads.

BARBER SHOP BALLOONS

Take balloons and inflate them tightly. Paint a face on them and put whipped cream on the face. Give the participants a straight-edge razor and have them shave the face of the balloon. The last one to pop his balloon wins.

BALLOON CATCH

The players are seated in a circle on the floor. Have them number off and send the one with the highest number to the center to be IT. IT holds a balloon which he suddenly drops at the same instant he calls a number. The player of that number tries to catch the balloon before it touches the floor. If he succeeds, IT tries again using another number. If he fails he becomes IT. Or, if he breaks the balloon when trying to catch it, he becomes IT. A few extra inflated balloons should be handy.

COLONEL BLIMP

This rigamarole is done with a tall glass of water. One person goes through an entire series of motions and words which others try to duplicate correctly the first time. The words and motions form a definite pattern. One who analyzes the pattern should not find them too difficult. The whole series includes three rounds. The second and third rounds are the same as the first, except that everything is done twice in the second round and three times in the third. Here is how it goes:

Pick up the glass between the thumb and one finger of the right hand saying, "Here's to the health of Colonel Blimp." Take one drink from the glass and set it down on the table with one distinct tap. Wipe the right side of an imaginary or real moustache with the right forefinger, then the left side with the left forefinger. Tap the table at the right of the glass with the right forefinger, then at the left with the left forefinger. Tap the underside of the table with the right forefinger and then with the left. Stamp on the floor with the right foot and then with the left. Rise a few inches from the chair and sit down again.

In the second round everything is by two like this: Pick up the glass between the thumb and two fingers saying, "Here's to the health of Colonel Blimp, Colonel Blimp." Take two drinks from the glass and set it down with two distinct taps. Wipe the right side of the moustache twice, and then the left side twice. Tap the table twice with the right forefinger and then twice with the left. Tap the underside of the table twice with right forefinger and then twice with the left. Stamp on the floor twice with the right foot and then twice with the left. Rise from the chair and sit down again twice.

On the third round, take the glass with thumb and three fingers, and say, "Here's to the health of Colonel Blimp, Colonel Blimp, Colonel Blimp," take three drinks, which must empty the glass, wipe the mouth three times with each forefinger, tap the top of the table and then the underside three times with each hand, stamp three times with each foot and rise from and sit down in the chair three times.

If an individual misses one part, his glass is filled again with water. Continue around the room, giving each person a turn. Come back to those who goofed and let them try, try, try again.   (HS)

BLOWING FOOTBALL

This game is always enjoyed and is played with much enthusiasm provided the table used approximates the proper dimensions. The table should be three to four feet wide and seven to eight feet long. A longer table makes scoring difficult and a shorter one is unsatisfactory from the health standpoint. Six inches from each end of the table and parallel to it draw a goal line with chalk. A Ping-Pong ball is used.

Divide the players into two teams. Teams of from four to eight players are most advantageous. The teams stand or kneel at opposite ends of the table. The team "kicking off" places the ball on the table one third of the distance from their goal to the opposite goal. The ball seesaws back and forth until one team succeeds in blowing it over the opponent's line. If it goes off the table over the side lines, it is placed in the center of the table opposite the point where it went out.

The players are not allowed to reach over their goal line with their mouths. They may get their heads together, however, and attempt to concentrate the force of their various blows. Most scoring is accomplished by allowing the ball to approach very close to the goal, then giving it a hard puff. In this way it can be sent forward with such momentum that the opponents will have difficulty in stopping it before it crosses their goal line.

The penalty for reaching over the goal line with the mouth is the giving of the ball to the opponents who place it three inches from their goal.

They then have an opportunity for an effective blow at the offender's goal. The offenders, however, are privileged to defend against the blow and attempt to stop the ball.

Each time the ball crosses the opponent's goal line a touchdown counting seven points is scored.

DRY RUN

Each team has a set of skis. These are made out of 2½-inch-thick boards, 6 feet long and 6 inches wide. The board is drilled with matching holes 15 inches apart.

Some sort of rope is needed to fasten the players' feet to the skis. Four people put one foot each on the skis and walk down the court and back. First team back wins. It's very difficult to get all working together at the same time to move the skis and should provide many laughs.   (HS)

EGG TOSS

Divide into two teams (guys against the gals makes for much excitement). Draw a dividing line and each player stands one big step from it. To start, each guy is given a raw egg, which he throws to the gal. Every time the egg is caught that couple takes one big step back. If the egg is missed, that couple is out of the game. The goal is to see who can stay in the game the longest and who can get back the farthest from the line.

THIEVES MARKET

Some objects of little value (penny, banana or paper clip) are given to each team, who in turn launch out into the community to trade their objects for something of increased value.

Rules:

1. The object cannot be returned to the home.
2. Must not be obtained from their own home or that of a friend.
3. Must be brought back within a specified time period.
4. All "treasures" are to become property of the youth group to be sold at a flea market or garage sale.

Winner is determined by the "treasure" having the greatest monetary value. Judges will be appointed and introduced before the game begins.   (HS)

BROOM HOCKEY

This game can be played with as many as 30 players per team. Each team is numbered in groups of 6 or whatever amount of brooms is provided for each team. To be fair, each team should number off boy-girl, boy-girl. If a team has 24 players it would have 4 sets of hockey players. Referee calls out numbers to play (1-6, 7-12, etc.) and when the whistle blows, the members called grab a broom (they must stay behind the goal line until the whistle blows) and try to hit the ball into the goal with the broom. If the ball goes out of bounds, it is thrown in. To give everybody a chance to play, each group of 6 plays until a score is made or their time is up (usually 3-5 minutes). The winner is the team with the most goals.

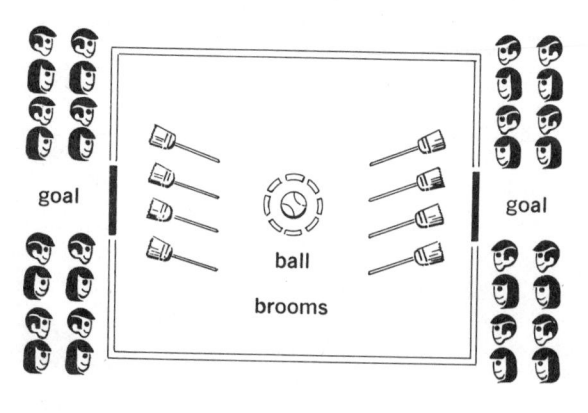

Outdoor Games

OUTDOOR GAMES

There are always some games that complement the outdoors.

To be successful, some care must be taken:

Place yourself in a position where everyone can hear the instructions.

Before beginning, double-check to see if there are any questions.

Do not allow the game to run beyond the group's peak of enthusiasm.

WELLS FARGO

Two teams are formed of any number of players with approximately the same physical strength and ratio of boys to girls. A captain is appointed for each team. One team is named the "Wells-Fargo Men" and players wear two-inch pieces of white adhesive tape on their foreheads.

The other team is called the "Indians" and players wear two-inch pieces of tape with a red dot on their foreheads. (The tapes are "scalps.")

A "bank" is established in a clear, level area by marking a circle six feet in diameter. The Wells-Fargo Men carry five bags or blocks of gold into the "bank" for fifteen points each. The Indians attempt to prevent the bank deposit and try to capture the gold and carry it into the "bank" themselves, thereby scoring fifteen points per bag for their team.

In addition to giving attention to the gold, both teams attempt to collect "scalps" from opponents by removing and keeping the pieces of tape, thereby scoring one point per scalp. A "scalped" player is dead and therefore out of the game. The following suggestions may be helpful.

1. A time limit may be set for the game or the game may be stopped at any time by the leaders in charge.

2. Ample time must be allowed before starting the game for team organization and strategy preparations.

3. Scalps and gold must be exposed to open view at all times.

4. Gold must be carried by a player into the "bank" circle. Score is counted only when both the gold and the player have completely entered the circle. Once a player has completely entered the circle, he cannot be removed by opposing players. A leader serving as "teller" receives the gold and keeps score.

5. At the conclusion of the game, players from each team bring scalps collected from opponents to their captain for scoring.

6. Boys may not fight girls either defensively or offensively. Only girls may scalp other girls or attack other girls carrying gold. Girls can tackle guys, but guys cannot tackle girls. Girls are free to attach boys for either gold or scalps.

7. Players are to exercise care to avoid personal injury to opponents or damage to clothing if at all possible. Players may be removed from the game at any time for unnecessary roughness.

GREASED WATERMELON

Throw a well-greased watermelon out into the water, not more than waist deep, and announce that the one who brings it in to shore first can have it. As a consolation prize for the many losers, be prepared to give each one of them a nice big slice out of another melon you have brought along.

ICE KEEP-AWAY

On a hot summer afternoon nothing will be quite so unique at a swimming party as a huge cake of ice. Choose up sides for a game of keep-away. Instead of using a beach ball, use the cake of ice. Your swimmers will have a great time as they try to keep the chilly elusive object away from each other.

PARACHUTE

A parachute twenty-four feet in diameter is surrounded by teens holding onto the outer edge.

Game #1

The group is numbered off from one to six. The parachute is laid on the ground with the youth still holding on to it. The leader counts to three and everyone stands and throws their hands above their heads, which makes the parachute balloon. The leader then calls out a number between one and six and the numbers called out must duck under the parachute and run to the opposite side. If they are caught under the chute they must stay there until the next number is called.

Game #2

The parachute is held in the same manner and a round ball is placed in the center of it. The object is to keep the ball from going over your head while trying to get it to bounce over the head of someone else. This is done by moving the chute up and down in a vigorous manner. When it goes over the head of someone they are out of the game.   (HS)

KROCHET

This game is a cross between football, soccer and baseball. It gives the unskilled and the girls as much opportunity as the athletic boys. The teams are equally divided.

The playing field is set up with three large posts, thirty-five feet apart, in a triangle. One post is the home post, one the pitcher's mound and the other first base. The pitcher must stand next to his post and roll the ball to home post, attempting to hit the post with the ball. The person who is up to bat can either kick the ball or hit it with the bat, which he must carry at all times, even when running down to first base and back. He can kick the ball anywhere in a 360-degree circle. He scores when he has completed a run around first base and back without the pitcher hitting the home post. Only the pitcher can roll the ball to the home post. The fielders always return the ball to the pitcher. The pitcher can roll the ball as many times as he has opportunity to before the runner returns from first base to kick it again. A batter continues to bat and run until he is put out by the ball striking home post. The batter can make several runs if the ball is hit far enough away. All fly balls caught are automatic outs. The teams exchange positions when an entire team has batted. The winner after two innings is the team with the most runs.

ESKIMO THROWING BLANKET

This idea comes from the national sport of the Eskimos. At one time they used it to locate seals on their flat tundra. A group of Eskimos tossed one person approximately fifty feet in the air. This person was able to spot seals a great distance away.

The Eskimo Throwing Blanket will bring years of fun to your group. It is a heavy round canvas, eight feet in diameter, with holders around the outer edge for a one-inch rope.

Up to twenty-four people can take hold of the rope around the edge, with one person seated in the middle.

The one riding the blanket MUST sit with legs apart, with hands holding the ankles, and the chin tucked to the chest. One person should be the counter, and count to three. On the first two counts rhythm is established by the holders, and on the count of three the rider is tossed into the air. I have seen them go as high as thirty feet. What a thrill! (HS)

(An Eskimo Throwing Blanket can be obtained by writing FUNTASTICS, 4364 Scottsfield Dr., San Jose, California 95123.)

BOD SQUAD

The object of this event is for the group to go out in the neighborhood and hunt for specific "bods," and bring them back alive to your meeting or party. The group is divided into teams and each is given a list of people to retrieve. Teams go out either on foot or in cars. Each team has thirty minutes to round up the "bods." No one counts who arrives at the meeting after the time limit is up. Award 100 points for each person found and brought in. People found do not have to stay, but just check in. A suggested list of bodies to hunt for:

1. Varsity football player
2. Student body officer
3. Exchange student (foreign)
4. Cheerleader
5. Girl with hair in rollers
6. Couple going steady
7. Boy in pajamas
8. Girl in swimsuit
9. Teacher
10. Someone who speaks Spanish
11. Boy with a Corvette
12. Student with a last name over ten letters
13. Twins
14. Boy in "jogging" outfit
15. Boy who owns a guinea pig
16. Girl with a capped tooth   (HS)

SAHARA DESERT

Divide the group in half. Each army chooses a captain. Both captains are then stranded on the Sahara Desert which is located 200-300 yards from the Suez Canal (water source). Each captain is holding an empty gallon container. Each team member is given a small paper cup. The object is to stop the other team before they get to the captain by spilling their water or throwing water all over them.

Rules:
1. Boys can block boys but not girls.
2. Girls can block both guys and girls.
3. Within two feet of the captain is a free zone and no combat can take place there.

4. It is best to have neutral people at the dam to fill the cups and have each team fill at opposite ends of the water source.

5. Distinguish teams with colored tape on their foreheads. (Or any other marking device.)

DUCK IN—DUCK OUT

Get several teams of five members each. Put each team in a separate rowboat and line the rowboats up evenly in a racing formation. Set up a finish line fifty yards down the course. At the signal each boat team is to propel themselves as well as possible using only their hands. (Oars are not allowed in the boat.) As the race progresses, the leader is to blow his whistle. Whenever the whistle is blown, all members of each team are to leap out of their boat into the water, climb back into the boat, wait until all members are in the boat, and then paddle on. Leaders are encouraged to blow their whistles often. After several times of "in-and-out," the boats swamp and the race becomes a real test of nautical skill.

THE STRIPPER RELAY

Get two or more teams of an equal number of participants. Obtain some baggy clothes (the funnier the better) for each team. Make sure that each team has similar clothing—shirts with buttons, pants with zippers. Place the clothes in individual team piles about twenty yards from the starting line on a raft or at the end of a pool. At the starting signal one member of each team swims to the raft or end of the pool, climbs out of the water, puts the clothes on, strips the clothes off and swims back to his team. He touches the next member of the team who then swims through the same process. The first team to finish the process wins.

ICE MELT

A twenty-five-pound block of ice is given to each team. A fifteen-minute time limit is set in which to melt the block of ice. No fire or water may be used. The winner is determined by weighing the blocks of ice.

Brain Teasers

BRAIN TEASERS

Everyone at your party will not be the athletic type. The games in this chapter will give your non-athletes an opportunity to show their ability and will provide a breather for the entire group.

There will also be those times when you will be at a loss because of a misplaced prop or because your help did not show up. This chapter provides some good ideas for fillers for those otherwise painful gaps.

It is important to swear to secrecy, all those who know or who guess the solution, both during and after the party. That way those who are stumped by the teaser will be propelled into action the next time you use it.

THE MYSTIC CANE

As a mystifying trick this one may appear weak, but it has been very successful for many years. Perhaps its popularity is due to the dramatic element and the action included in it. The mind reader tries to guess some simple action verb that the others have selected and to indicate the correctness of his guess by acting out the verb. His confederate makes remarks, gives instructions and taps on the floor with a cane.

The selected verb is spelled out by the confederate in a very simple code. Each consonant is indicated by using it as the initial letter of the second word in a statement. Each vowel is indicated by a certain number of taps on the floor with a cane—one tap for **a,** two for **e,** three for **i,** four for **o,** and five for **u.** For example, suppose the selected word is "write." The confederate might say, "I wish you would all concentrate." Then, after a pause long enough to indicate a new statement, "Get ready now." Then tap, tap, tap with the cane to indicate **i.** Next, "It takes cooperation of all of you to make this a success," and finally, tap, tap—**e.** The mind reader is now ready to take a pencil and paper and begin writing.

THE MYSTERIOUS CHINESE WRITING

Two persons must have complete understanding of this mysterious chirography. One goes out of the room, the other remains and asks the company to select some word to be written. Pretend "cat" is the word chosen. The reader is called back. The writer uses a pointed pencil or stick of wood to make various maneuvers on the floor, wall or table. The reader watches intently.

"Can you follow me?" asks the writer after a bit of this mysterious maneuvering. After more of this he taps once, then with a grand flourish finishes up saying, "That's all." Immediately the reader says "cat."

The consonants are given by what is said, the first letter in the sentence indicates the letter. Thus, when the writer says, "Can you follow me?" the other immediately knows that the letter is **c.** The vowels are **a,e,i,o,u.** Therefore 1,2,3,4 and 5 taps indicate which vowel is to be used.

The more mysterious you can make your maneuvering with the pointer, the better. Although it has nothing to do with your writing of the word, it is to your advantage to make them think it has. We have seen a company completely mystified by this stunt. If anyone thinks he has gotten it, let him go out and then come back and read the word selected. Often players will guess the consonants, but are unable to fathom your vowel system.

SUPER MIND-READING STUNT

This is a fascinating stunt. The group selects a well-known person, fictional, living or dead. The leader transmits the name to the accomplice by signals. All signals are seen or heard by the group but few persons can figure out the trick when they see it for the first time, or for that matter, for the tenth time.

In the first place, the actual name of the person selected is never transmitted unless there is no other way of informing the accomplice. The leader gives leads that are words associated with the selected name. It is up to the accomplice to put these words of association together and to figure out from them the identity of the person selected.

Suppose the person selected by the group was Eve Curie. The leader could give one word of association and the accomplice could guess that. "Radium" would do the trick. The word "radium" would be spelled out to the accomplice.

The spelling is done this way. The consonants are given by taking the accomplice "on a trip." The first letters of the cities mentioned are the consonants in the word being spelled. Thus, to spell "radium" the leader might start the trip at **Rochester.**

The vowels are given in a different way. This is always confusing to the listeners. The vowels are numbered as they appear in the alphabet. **A** is one, **e** is two, **i** is three, **o** is four, **u** is five. While taking a trip to **Rochester** we stopped for **one** night. That gives the **r** and **a** in "radium." From Rochester we go to **D**enver, giving the **d.** We stay in Denver **three** nights and **five** days, giving the **i** and the **u.** We finish the trip in **M**emphis. This gives us the final **m.**

If the accomplice fails to guess, a new clue may be given. Where more than one word is used, a changed method of transportation indicates the break between the words. Leader says: "Let's take a train from there," or "We go by plane to Memphis."   (HS)

BLACK MAGIC

The leader must have an accomplice in this event. The accomplice boasts that he can leave the room and upon returning name any object that the players selected in his absence.

When the accomplice is out of the room the players select an object. When the accomplice is recalled, the leader then names one article after another saying, "Is it . . . .?" He finally names the selected article and the accomplice says, "Yes, that is it." The correct article is the one the leader names immediately after he names a black article or one nearly black.

FAKE TEMPLE READING

A leader leaves the room while the others select any number no greater than ten. The leader returns and places his fingers on the temples of each player, one after another, in an effort to learn the selected number. Emphasize that the players are to try not to reveal the number, but it is explained that some of them will probably do so in spite of themselves. In fact, one of the players who is confederate of the leader actually reveals the number by contracting his biting muscles the appropriate number of times. The leader counts the number of bites to determine the number. This part is the same as in the standard mind-reading game.

When the leader learns the number he proceeds as if nothing happened until he comes to the victim. He concentrates closely while touching the victim's temples and then announces the number. He claims to have learned it from the victim. (HS)

NINE BOOKS TRICK

Nine books are laid out on the floor, three rows of three in each row. The leader and his accomplice know the trick. While the accomplice is out of the room, the group chooses one of the books. The accomplice, reentering the room, is asked by the leader who is pointing at a book, "Is this the one?"

The accomplice answers "no" on the wrong books and "yes" on the right one.

Repeat until someone says he knows the trick, then give him a chance to prove it. Have him do it several times. He might get the right one the first time just by luck.

The trick is a simple one. The books have a definite position. There are the top left corner, top center and top right. The center row contains center left, center center and center right. The bottom row contains lower left, lower center and lower right. The correct book is indicated by the leader on the first point. With his stick or cane, he points to any book and says, "Is this the one?" The place he points on the book indicates which book has been selected. If he is pointing to the upper left corner of any book, the accomplice then does not answer in the affirmative until the leader points to the upper left book. If, however,

the leader is pointing to the upper left book and the upper left corner on the first point, the accomplice immediately answers "yes."

The leader can confuse the audience by changing tactics and questions: "Is it this one? Is it that one? Is this the one?" The watchers are confused into thinking it is the words or how they are spoken that makes the difference. The player who thinks he knows the trick is often caught when the leader points to the correct book on the first point.

BLIND VISION

Each player writes a word, a phrase or a short sentence on a slip of paper, folds the slip and deposits it in a container. The mind reader takes one of the slips and without unfolding it, presses it against his forehead. He then announces what is on the slip and asks for the writer to identify himself. One of the players will admit to writing it. The mind reader unfolds the slip and reads it for confirmation. He then goes through the same procedure with the second slip. He takes the slips one after another and reads them all, simply by holding each folded slip to his forehead.

The secret is in the method of handling the first slip. The one held to the mind reader's forehead is an authentic one written by a player who is not in on the secret. The words spoken by the mind reader are not the ones on the slip at all, but words agreed upon in advance with a confederate. In fact, it is not necessary to have a sentence agreed upon, but only an understanding that the confederate will acknowledge authorship of whatever words the mind reader reads first.

When the mind reader looks at the first slip "for confirmation," he is actually learning what is written on it. Then when he holds the second slip to his head and pretends to read it, he actually calls out the words appearing on the first one. He continues pretending to read the words on a slip but actually calling the words on the preceding one.

If the confederate contributes a slip like everyone else, the mind reader's system will be disrupted when he reaches this slip. It is best for the confederate not to contribute a slip at all. If this method is used the game will have to be halted before all slips are read. Otherwise, the players will notice that one slip is missing. Another possibility is that the confederate's slip be made identifiable and be taken from the container last.

EYES IN THE BACK OF MY HEAD

This stunt is really baffling to one who does not know the method. There is no confederate or accomplice used and no trick method of communication as in the usual magic stunt.

The performer says that he can turn his back and tell anyone which hand he put up over his head. Someone is sure to ask for a demonstration. The performer seats this person at a table and tells him to lay his hands on it, palms down. The performer turns his back and says, "Now hold one hand up over your head." The player does this. The leader says, "If you have your hand over your head cross your feet." This the player does also. Then the leader says, "If your feet are crossed put your hand on the table."

The player lays his hand on the table and the performer turns around, glances at the hands, looks under the table, examines the crossed feet and then points out the hand that was raised.

The secret is that the hand which was held over the head will be slightly pale compared to the natural color of the other hand. This may sound dumb to you, but try it—it works!

Having the player cross his feet serves two purposes. It consumes time, keeping the player's hand in the air, and confuses the spectators to keep them from guessing how the trick was done.

LEGS

While the mind reader is out of the room, the other players select any object in the room, such as a table, a rug or a lamp. When the mind reader returns, he is asked questions by his confederate and identifies the selected object.

The code is in the first questions asked by the confederate and the mind reader needs only to note whether this question refers to an object with legs. If it does, then the next time the confederate refers to an object with legs, the mind reader will know that this is the one selected. If the first question refers to an object without legs, the selected object will be the next one without legs mentioned by the confederate. For example, if the selected object is a certain chair, the confederate may point to a table and say, "Is it this?" Then he points to a lamp and other objects without legs. Finally he points to the selected chair and the mind reader says that it is the selected object. (HS)

LEVITATION

This stunt gives your guests the impression that you have practiced mass hypnotic suggestion on them, but really it is done without any hypnosis.

Ask one of the guys at the party to act as a subject for an experiment in levitating, or defeating the law of gravity. Assure him that he will not be harmed in the least but will be gently lifted into the air on the fingertips of five pretty girls. Have your subject sit in a straightbacked, armless chair.

Now choose five girls who stand two on each side of the subject and one in front. Each girl clasps her hands before her with index fingers extended, tips together. Tell the guy to sit up straight, head slightly bowed and hands folded in his lap while he concentrates on rising effortlessly and floating above his chair. Now the girls place the tips of their fingers in five strategic positions; under the subject's chin, under each knee and each armpit.

At a signal from you, all the girls are to take a deep breath and simultaneously li-i-ft up the man. Up he goes, several inches above his seat. Up he remains for a second or two and down he floats onto his chair again. If by chance the stunt doesn't succeed the first time, it is because the girls didn't concentrate hard enough—or, to be more exact, one of them is off in her timing. Just try again and again until the girls succeed.

The girls can do this stunt as often as they want, provided they work together with precision timing. The stunt is especially funny if, after the timing is perfected, you choose a very big man for the subject.

Levitation seems mystical, but actually the strength of the girls' fingers is sufficient to perform the feat. The man's weight is divided among five girls and the upward force is placed at just the right spots.   (HS)

RED, WHITE AND BLUE

This trick, on the order of Black Magic, is difficult to solve.

When the accomplice is recalled the leader names one article after another and the accomplice is able to pick out the correct article by the following scheme: The first time he comes in it is the first article named after something red is named. The second time it is after something white and the third time after something blue.

If anyone thinks he has it figured out, let him try it.   (HS)

MIND READING

The leader states that he can tell the owner of any object just by holding it in his hand. (He does not point out that he has a confederate.) He then leaves the room. When he returns he is given an object furnished by a person the group selects. His confederate says, "Knock down the answer, Professor." He immediately guesses Karen Davis from the initials of the first two words in the sentence. (HS)

GRANDMOTHER'S TEA

The players are seated in a circle. The leader says, "My grandmother likes coffee but she doesn't like tea." This statement is best made with no preliminary explanation at all. The leader just makes it as a casual remark. Perhaps some of those present will know the game. If not, it will be apparent that each of the others is to make a statement similar to that of the leader. They will say such things as, "My grandmother likes peaches, but she doesn't like cream," or "She likes cabbage, but she doesn't like lettuce." (The first of these examples would be rejected, but the other accepted.) Frequently a player will make an acceptable statement purely by accident, thus adding to the mystery. It finally becomes clear to all that grandmother does not like the letter **T** and hence she does not like any food that has this letter in its name. She likes peas, cabbage, okra, bread and many other things. But she simply cannot stand potatoes, carrots, peanuts or butter.

MONEY MAGIC

In the leader's absence an assistant asks the group to choose any number up to 156. They choose 137. The assistant places a nickel on a magazine; then places a penny near it. The leader is called back, looks at the coins and says, "137."

If a leader and his assistant withhold clues a group can be kept guessing for months. But, the more social approach is deliberately to let the group get the first clue after a few rounds. Make it apparent that the face of a clock furnishes the basic plan for the placing of the coins.

Here's the solution: The figures on the face of a clock determine the position of each coin. When the nickel is heads up, square the number under it. When the nickel shows tails, do not square the number under it. When the penny is heads up, add the number under it to the sum of the number under the nickel. When the penny shows tails, subtract the number under it from the sum of the number under the nickel. (HS)

GOING TO EUROPE

Each one says that he is going to Europe and taking a certain item with him. The leader tells him whether or not he can go. After a little while, each one catches on to the fact that the item must begin with a certain letter or two letters to be acceptable. A good way to choose the letters is to have each person bring something starting with his first and last initials.

I KNOW

The leader announces that any player who knows the right thing may become a member of the "I Know Club." He says, "I know football and that admits me." Each of the others in turn tells what he knows. If one says he knows sports or trees or carpentry, he is courteously admitted to the club. But one who claims to know medicine, athletics or agriculture is refused membership. The players are to guess what it is that admits some and keeps others out. They eventually learn, perhaps with a few pointed hints, that they must know something the name of which does not contain the letter I.   (HS)

SPOON PHOTOGRAPHY

Players sit in a circle. The photographer leaves the room and one of the players is chosen to have "his likeness took." The players also choose someone from the crowd to hold the spoon in front of this person for a moment, handing it to the photographer on his return. The photographer polishes the bowl of the spoon, passes it around and reflects several faces in the bowl. Finally he names the one chosen in his absence, stopping when that person's face is reflected in the spoon. A confederate assumes the exact posture of the player chosen. The photographer, of course, pretends to see the image in the spoon.

Relays

RELAYS

Most relay races are identical with simple races except that the players form teams and the members of each team take turns in performing the same activity.

Repetition can have a poor effect if there is little humor in it. Therefore, use relays sparingly. At the most, three at one party.

MAGNETISM

This is a relay which will produce many laughs. Divide the group into two or more teams depending on the number of people present. Each player is given a straw. The lead person on each team is also given a small piece of Kleenex or other cleansing tissue. By drawing in his breath the leader can hold the tissue on the end of his straw. The next teammate puts his straw against the tissue and draws in his breath. The lead person then releases his breath. The idea is to pass the tissue to each member of the team. If the paper falls on the floor, it must be picked up the same way, by drawing breath through the straw.

The team which finishes first wins. If there are only a few people playing, then the tissue can be passed back in reverse.

LOADED MOUSETRAPS

Have a member of each team carry a loaded mousetrap to a certain line and back and hand it the next player without springing it. It is a frightening experience and often the traps will snap! If this happens the player carrying it must start over.

MATCHBOX RELAY

For this active and comical relay, divide the group into two teams. Give one member of each team a wooden cover from a safety matchbox.

The object of the game is to start with the matchbox cover pinched over your nose and pass it on to the nose of another member of your team —without using hands! The matchbox cover fits over your nose if you hold your head back.

If there are only a few players on each team, the matchbox can go progressively from the first to the last person and then back again to the first nose.

If the box drops to the floor you may have two chances to pick it up with your nose. If you can't, then you can pick it up with your hands and place it on your nose.　(HS)

PAPER ROLL

Divide the group into two teams and place two single-file lines side by side. Give each line a roll of toilet paper and the following instructions: Unwrap the roll of tissue paper and hold the end, passing it over the heads of those in back of you. When the roll gets to the end of the line, that person passes it up to the person in front of him and it goes until it reaches the front of the line. This process is repeated until all the paper is off the roll.

POWDER PUFF DERBY

Any old V.W. will do. A wide stretch of beach or unused dirt road and a stop watch are needed, too. Place one gal behind the wheel of the car and have as many fellas "behind" the car as can fit around it. At the shout of "go" they are off. Have them go to a stated point and then return to the starting line. A litle hill coming back makes it interesting.　(HS)

TOOTHPICK AND LIFESAVER RELAY

Teams line up. Everybody has a toothpick in their mouths and they try to pass a lifesaver down the line without using their hands.　(HS)

INNER TUBE RELAY

Each team chooses ten couples (two boys or two girls—each couple must be the same sex). Each pair runs from the team corner to the team inner tube. Both must squeeze through the inner tube at the same time, starting with the top of the body and working down. The first team to have all ten pairs finished wins.   (HS)

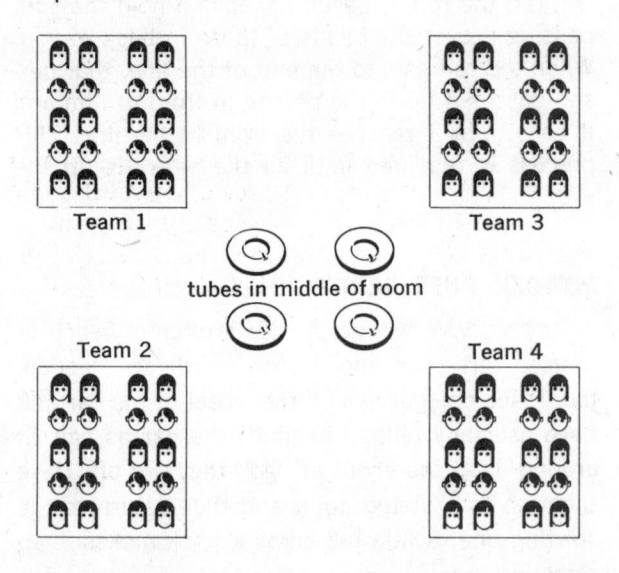

Team 1

Team 3

tubes in middle of room

Team 2

Team 4

TELEPHONE DIRECTORY RELAY

Players are divided into relay teams and identical copies of a telephone directory are given to each team. The leader prepares in advance identical lists of page numbers each accompanied by another number. The second number is not greater than ten. Each team is given one of the lists. At a signal the first player of each team opens his directory to the page indicated by the first number on the list. In the right-hand column of this page he counts down the number of entries as indicated by the second number that accompanies the page number. Having found the indicated entry, he writes its telephone number on a sheet of paper. Then he hands list, directory and sheet of paper to the second man on his team. Proceeding in the same way, the second man finds the second telephone number and writes it down. The same process is repeated for the other numbers by the other players. This is continued until every player has found and written down a telephone number. The first team to produce a complete and accurate list is the winner. (HS)

SNOWFIGHT

Two teams are separated by a row of chairs and given a six-foot stack of newspaper. They are given one minute to wad the paper up. When the signal is given each team attempts to throw the most paper on the other team's side by the time limit. Each round (usually about four rounds per party) is separated by a thirty-second break to find everyone who might be buried in the mountain of paper. The team with the most paper on their side loses. However, there is always such a mess that a tie is declared. Give paper to an ecology drive afterwards.

Caution: The only way to stop the throwing between rounds is to give each person who throws something a good penalty.

BUMPER-BOX RELAY

A member from each team is covered with a refrigerator box. When the signal is given, each person is to run to the opposite wall, touch it with the box and turn back. He cannot lift the box. Hilarious results occur because the contestants cannot tell where they are going.   (HS)

FOREHEAD RACE

Couples run between two points with an object between their foreheads. (Grapefruit or water balloon.)

GRAPEFRUIT PASS

Couples attempt to pass a grapefruit between each other while in a sitting position. The grapefruit is held under the chin. No hands are to be used. If the grapefruit is dropped, both get penalized.

ESKINOSE

Divide the group into two teams, alternating by sex. First person has lipstick smeared on his nose. The winning team is the one which can pass the lipstick the farthest in thirty seconds by Eskimo kissing.

BOTTLE-FILL RELAY

Each team appoints one boy to lay down face up with his head toward the starting line and holding an empty pop bottle on his head. Each team member fills a cup (made of unbendable material) with water, runs to the bottle and pours in water until it is gone. He then runs back and as soon as he crosses the starting line, the next contestant runs out with a cup of water. The first team to fill the bottle wins.

coke bottle
on head

pail of water

107

A T.P. RIP

This is a good game for any place you might be. Each team selects eight teens who take part in the following manner. One guy walks backwards toward a goal (fifty feet away) unrolling a roll of toilet paper. Another guy follows him with a pair of scissors and cuts the unrolled paper in half lengthwise without tearing it apart. Two more kids follow and cut the two halves in half. All three players must be careful not to tear the toilet paper. Subtract points for each tear. Four more teens come behind rolling the four strips back into rolls. The first team to reach goal with four narrow, separate rolls wins!

ICE CUBE SURPRISE

Organize two or more teams and line up each team with one player in back of the other. Give the last man of each team a table knife. Then give the first player of each an ice cube. Don't tell him what you are giving him—let it be a surprise! This is part of the game.

The first player, without turning around, hands it back to the second player in line. The second hands it to the third and so on. The last man in the line takes the ice cube, places it on his knife, races to a line 25 feet behind him and then runs back. When he returns he passes the ice cube and knife to the next player. This player must run to the line and back. Each player gets a chance to run while balancing an ice cube. If the cube drops, the runner must pick it up with his knife.

The first team to finish wins. Be sure you start with big-sized ice cubes and small teams if it is a hot day.

In announcing the game, say: "Your team will be given an object to pass through to each player. The last man must run to the 25-foot line in back of him with the object on his knife and return the object to the team." In this way, the ice cube will really be a surprise.   (HS)

IRISH CONFETTI RELAY

Players form two lines, standing opposite each other. The leader of each line has ten stones of varying sizes on a chair beside him. All players link arms. At a signal the leader picks up one of the stones between his two index fingers and passes it down the line. The other stones follow in as rapid succession as possible. Everyone uses only the index fingers of both hands. Arms are never unlinked. If a stone falls, it must be retrieved with the help of the entire line, for linked arms will reach just so far and no farther. The line wins which passes all the stones to the end first.

CHARIOT RACE

This spectacular race is a favorite with junior highers, especially after the "Chariot Drivers" develop sufficient skill to pick up the handkerchief with the "Horses" stopping as they make the turn.

Divide the players into groups of five. Each group chooses one of its members to take his place on a blanket held at each corner by the acting horses. Arrange the horses and drivers behind a starting line. Each team sets up a handkerchief in wigwam fashion on the goal line and all is ready for the word "go."

Action. When the signal is given the chariots race to the goal line. As they approach the handkerchief the Horses slow down to make a turn around the handkerchief. As he passes the handkerchief, the driver picks it up with his teeth. The chariots then race back to the starting line which is now the finish line.

Winner. The chariot wins that crosses the finish line first, provided no player lost his grip on either the blanket or the hanky.

Notes for Leaders. Unless a great amount of space is available, this race must be run in heats since it requires so much space for each chariot to turn.

When time doesn't permit running the race in heats make it a straightaway race and erect the handkerchief half-way between the start and finish lines.